HOW DRONES WILL IMPACT SOCIETY

by John Hakala

ReferencePoint Press®

San Diego, CA

TECHNOLOGY'S IMPACT

ReferencePoint Press®

Printed in the United States

For more information, contact:
ReferencePoint Press, Inc.
PO Box 27779
San Diego, CA 92198
www.ReferencePointPress.com

LIBRARY OF CONGRESS CATALOGING-IN-PUBLICATION DATA

Name: Hakala, John, 1989– author.
Title: How Drones Will Impact Society / by John Hakala.
Description: San Diego, CA : ReferencePoint Press, Inc., [2019] | Series: Technology's Impact | Includes bibliographical references and index. | Audience: Grades 9 to 12.
Identifiers: LCCN 2018011544 (print) | LCCN 2018013170 (ebook) | ISBN 9781682824948 (ebook) | ISBN 9781682824931 (hardback)
Subjects: LCSH: Drone aircraft—Juvenile literature.
Classification: LCC TL685.35 (ebook) | LCC TL685.35 .H35 2019 (print) | DDC 629.133/39—dc23
LC record available at https://lccn.loc.gov/2018011544

Contents

IMPORTANT EVENTS IN THE DEVELOPMENT OF **DRONE TECHNOLOGY**

1800 | 1875 | 1900 | 1925 | 1950 | 2000

1849
Austrians use hot-air balloons to bomb Venice, Italy.

1903
The Wright brothers make four flights at Kitty Hawk, North Carolina.

1918
The Kettering Bug aerial torpedo flies without a pilot.

1936
The first practical helicopter flies in Germany.

1973
Israel develops the first unmanned surveillance drone.

1982
Israel wins an air battle against Syria using unmanned aerial vehicles.

1985
The United States begins the mass production of drones.

1995
The RQ-1 drone is developed by General Atomics for reconnaissance.

2002
The RQ-1 Predator drone is weaponized as the MQ-1 model.

2005
Recovery teams use drones to find survivors of Hurricane Katrina.

2010
Smartphones can control drones.

2011
The United States performs a controversial drone strike on a US citizen in Yemen.

2013
The drone company DJI creates a camera-mounted drone.

2015
Drones begin inspecting Minnesota roads and bridges.

2016
The first known nonmilitary drone-related death occurs.

2017
The first drone collision with a passenger aircraft occurs in Canada.

2018
The Chinese company Ehang successfully tests passenger drone flights.

2000 2005 2010 2015 2020

Drones to the Rescue

Ocean currents create dangerous conditions for swimmers and surfers. In January 2018, two teenagers were struggling for survival in turbulent waters off the coast of New South Wales, Australia. A quick response time by rescuers was critical for their survival. Fortunately, a lifeguard team was equipped with a state-of-the-art flying robot called a drone.

The drone, called Little Ripper, was immediately dispatched to rescue the swimmers. Attached to this unmanned aircraft was an inflatable raft. The drone reached the teenagers in just seventy seconds. It then deployed the raft, which allowed them to safely return to shore. Lifeguard supervisor Jai Sheridan stated, "On a normal day that would have taken our lifeguards a few minutes longer."[1] When seconds can mean the difference between life and death, a drone like Little Ripper becomes a valuable tool for rescue teams.

Not only does this drone deploy safety equipment, it is also equipped with sensors and **algorithms** that detect sharks in the water. It is a brand-new, highly versatile aerial lifeguard that may soon be patrolling many beaches worldwide. "The applications in the water are just phenomenal," said University of Technology Sydney professor Michael Blumenstein.[2] Drones are quickly becoming useful for many sectors, including business, government, and personal recreation. The adaptability and diversity of these aerial robots have shaped the impact drones have on society.

There are many models and purposes for drones. They have become a part of both business and recreation.

THE DRONES HAVE LANDED

Drones are found in many areas of modern life. In the United Kingdom, delivery drones are already passing through the sky fulfilling orders. It might not be too long before these flying aircraft replace standard forms of delivery. Major online retailers are already developing and testing drones to deliver goods on demand. Even fast-food chains are beginning to fly customer orders aboard drones.

> **WORDS IN CONTEXT**
>
> **algorithm**
> A programmed set of rules a computer uses to solve a problem.

All drones can fly, but beyond that, their functions can vary widely depending on how they are used. One of the most popular attachments is the camera. Drones are now commonly used by the entertainment industry to capture incredible views for movies, television shows, and sporting events. "We're getting shots you wouldn't get any other way," says Aerial Mob cofounder Tony Carmean.[3] Aerial photography is also changing the approach realtors take to sell houses and the way utility companies inspect their vital equipment and resources.

The military is one of the most widely recognized users of drone technology. Highly sophisticated multimillion-dollar drones prowl the skies. These drones often fly high above the clouds, out of detectable reach of the enemy. Some military drones simply collect intelligence in the form of photos and video. Others strike enemy targets with missiles and bombs. While the military argues that replacing piloted aircraft with drones saves lives and resources, the use of drones has highly vocal critics. American **cognitive** scientist Noam Chomsky says, "A drone strike is a terror weapon, [but] we don't talk about it that way."[4]

WORDS IN CONTEXT

cognitive
Relating to the mind gaining knowledge through experiences and senses.

Government agencies also use drones for nonmilitary purposes. Natural resources are protected and monitored with unmanned aircraft. Drones assist in the fighting of devastating wildfires. Critical roads and bridges are also now closely inspected by photography drones to make the country safer to navigate.

Although harmful or negative things can happen when people misuse drones or ignore safety regulations and standards, the future

Drone technology will be able to impact many sectors of the economy. Industries from home security to delivery could be affected.

may bring overwhelmingly positive innovations. It is up to society to determine the future of drones.

THE FLYING FUTURE

While there are many examples of drone use today, much of the promise lies in the future. Advances in delivery services are transforming the field of medicine. Industry leaders are already at work on systems in which lifesaving blood, supplies, and even transplantable organs are safely and quickly delivered by drones.

With the increase in number of drones, the future holds many possibilities for the technology. The world will have to adjust to a new wave of ideas.

The inspiration for human flight came from observing animals in the sky. Inspiration for futuristic drone designs and applications also comes from animals and nature.

The military is always looking to evolve defense technology. The United States Air Force is researching how peregrine falcons hunt prey in the air to help remove threats like rogue drones. Safety is also in mind when geology and volcano experts team up to do extensive volcano research. Flying drones near active or erupting volcanoes allows scientists to capture vital information about hazardous volcanoes. Farmers and plant lovers everywhere are troubled by the rapid decrease of the bee population. Drones could someday help solve the problems this decline creates.

Drones have the potential to bring huge changes to daily life. Even the dream of the flying car is becoming reality thanks to drone manufacturers. Successful test flights are already showing that people can be safely transported. Companies are even including drones in some home security services.

Some people worry about the government's use of drones. "Drones make surveillance cheaper and easier, and when you do that, you can expect to see a lot more of it," says University of Washington law professor Ryan Calo.[5] Some experts view drones as great national security tools, while others are fearful that having more cameras in the sky will invade the privacy of law-abiding citizens. Only time will tell how big of an impact these unmanned aerial vehicles (UAVs) will have, despite their lifesaving possibilities.

Chapter 1

What Is the Technology Behind Drones?

Drone technology is becoming widely available to the public. Today, people can simply pick a drone off the shelf at the store and bring it home. Drones are also easily purchased online. But, historically speaking, it was not long ago that a flying machine designed for human use was merely a fantasy. The rapid advancement in aviation technology is often taken for granted. To be able to fully appreciate modern drone technology, it is important to understand how drone technology started and how far it has come.

DAWN OF THE DRONES

Drones, or UAVs, do not require a human pilot onboard when they fly. UAVs used for practical purposes are traced back to 1849. The Austrian military used balloons rigged with explosives to assault Venice, Italy, in history's first use of unmanned aerial warfare. The balloons were set adrift in the wind to try to bomb the city of Venice. Many of the balloons did not reach the city, but Venice surrendered two days later.

The two World Wars spurred innovation in drone technology. During World War I (1914–1918), allied forces from France and Britain were the first to use aerial photography. This idea went on to be an extremely important purpose for UAVs. In 1917, the United States created a flying bomb known as the Kettering Bug to hit targets up

Drones have become incredibly popular for children and adults. Even though children can fly them, there are still safety concerns.

to 40 miles (64 km) away. They were not known for accuracy. "You'd launch them into some area, like a city, where they're bound to hit something," said Bart Everett, author of a 2015 book about the history of drone warfare.[6] However, the war ended before any of the Bugs were used in battle, and eventually production ceased.

In the 1940s, thousands of radio-controlled planes were produced for the US Army by Reginald Denny's Radioplane Company. During World War II (1939–1945), these pilotless planes were frequently used as target practice for antiaircraft gunners. Army and navy gunners sharpened their shooting skills by taking out the unmanned aircraft.

The second half of the twentieth century saw the greatest technological leaps in the field of UAVs. In 1973, Israel created the first unpiloted surveillance vehicle, called the Mastiff UAV. In 1982,

Drones have become incredibly common in today's culture. They are on television and in stores.

the Israeli Air Force used UAVs as decoys in a battle against Syria's air force to eliminate Syria's surface-to-air missiles. Not only did the Israelis win the battle, their casualties were also minimized because they had destroyed the Syrian missiles. The 1980s saw more drone development in the United States as well. In 1984, Leading Systems Inc. created the Amber drone for the US government. Amber was a surveillance drone capable of flying for thirty-eight hours straight. Before this drone was officially deemed operational, production was stopped in 1990 for budgetary reasons. However, Amber's creator, Abe Karem, used this design to create the famous Predator drone for General Atomics that revolutionized the drone and military world in 1995. The Predator's advances in flight time, surveillance, and eventually combat ability from half the world away allowed for UAVs to take on a much larger role.

After Hurricane Katrina hit in 2005, many communities in the southern United States were devastated. In Mississippi, the University of South Florida's Center for Robot-Assisted Search and Rescue (CRASAR) used small drones to help look for survivors. CRASAR director Dr. Robin Murphy said, "It takes too long for manned helicopters to get there."[7] Dr. Murphy said, "If you told me in 2005, having seen their clear value after Katrina, that it would be 10 years before they were adopted by all of the emergency management systems, I would have laughed."[8] It wasn't until May 2006 that the military-grade Predator drones were officially permitted by the Federal Aviation Administration (FAA) to fly through civilian airspace for search-and-rescue missions. The Predator and its successor, the Reaper, are equipped with **infrared** cameras that allow authorities to detect the heat signatures of people or animals. After seeing how these powerful drones could help, some believe they should have been authorized sooner.

WORDS IN CONTEXT

infrared
A type of radiation invisible to humans.

The private-use UAV industry took off. Launched in 2010, the Parrot AR.Drone was a breakthrough device that could be controlled by a smartphone. The company DJI released the popular Phantom UAV in 2013, which was one of the first that allowed users to mount small GoPro action cameras to it. This created an enormous demand for hobby and commercial uses. Companies began to speculate on ways drones could be used to help their businesses. FAA permits were issued to film companies, which could now afford to shoot movies and television shows that previously would have required an expensive helicopter.

Thrust and lift are key components to get any aircraft flying. Different kinds of aircraft deal with thrust and lift in different ways.

Innovations continue to roll out at a rapid pace. Many consumers now have access to increasingly sophisticated aerial devices. DJI vice president Paul Xu notes, "We are transforming this from a hobby to a profession."[9] While the uses of UAVs vary, it is remarkable how far humans have come in a short period of time. What was once an unguided hot-air balloon has become a key tool for movie production. Knowing how a drone operates makes it much easier to design unique and exciting future applications.

THE BASICS OF FLIGHT

The primary objective of any drone is to fly. Understanding the main forces that allow different types of drones to fly is key to understanding what drones do on basic level. The four forces of flight are thrust, lift, drag, and gravity. All these forces apply to both major types of aircraft: fixed-wing aircraft and rotorcraft. Fixed-wing aircraft typically have a large, rigid wing in a fixed position. Examples include airliners, fighter jets, and drones like the Predator. Rotorcraft instead have one or more large rotors, or downward-facing propellers. Examples include helicopters and drones like the Parrot.AR and the Phantom.

Thrust is what makes the aircraft work. Thrust is provided by an aircraft's engines. It gives the aircraft forward movement. Some aircraft use a jet engine for this. Others use spinning propellers. In helicopters, thrust is generated instead by a large propeller called a rotor. It pushes air straight downward. This pushes the helicopter up into the sky. Many common types of drones have multiple rotors that work in a similar way.

The second major force involved in flight is lift. In fixed-wing aircraft, the wings are designed to be shapes called airfoils. Airfoils typically have a rounded leading edge, a sharp trailing edge, and a curved design in the middle. They are designed so that air moves faster on top of the wing than it does below the wing. This creates a difference in air pressure, leading to what is known as **Bernoulli's principle**. The pressure pushing up on the wing is greater than the pressure pushing down. The wing is pushed upward, giving the aircraft lift.

> **WORDS IN CONTEXT**
>
> **Bernoulli's principle**
> A principle in physics that states that as air's speed increases, its pressure decreases.

The third major force of flight is drag. Drag is the force that opposes thrust. The main cause of drag is the air resistance that the aircraft faces as it flies. Air molecules push back against the aircraft as it flies through them, slowing the vehicle down. The bulkier the aircraft, the more drag it experiences. This is why modern fighter jets are designed with a sleek profile. This reduces the drag they experience and allows them to fly faster and more efficiently.

Gravity is the fourth force acting upon all aircraft. It counters lift in airplanes and vertical thrust in helicopters. Gravity pulls objects with mass toward each other. The more massive the object, the more gravitational pull it has. Earth, as an enormous object, pulls all objects that are near it toward the planet's center. This includes aircraft. For aircraft, the force of lift must be greater than the force of gravity for the vehicle to remain in the air.

PROVIDING THE POWER

Like other types of aircraft, drones require a power source to provide thrust. There are six major ways to power a drone. Each method has advantages and disadvantages.

The most common power source in consumer drones is a lithium battery. This source of power is readily available and relatively cheap. The batteries can be easily recharged or replaced when necessary. The disadvantage of battery power is the relatively short life. This limitation makes it necessary to land the drone frequently to recharge, making long flights difficult or impossible.

A second source of energy, currently only utilized by experimental winged drones, is solar power. With this method, solar panels are directly attached to the wings. When the sun is out, the solar panels harvest the energy and store it in a battery. The drone draws upon the battery reserves when the sun is absent. The advantage is that these devices fly for a much longer period of time. This was demonstrated

Solar panels have been added to some drones in order to keep them charged. Drones that use solar panels can stay airborne for much longer than most drones.

by the company Atlantik Solar. The company flew a solar-powered drone for eighty-one consecutive hours. The current disadvantages are cost and decreased efficiency with heavier drones.

Hydrogen fuel-cell power is a new method that has been researched and tested. A hydrogen fuel cell lasts much longer than batteries. This technology has been tested on the DJI Matrice 100 drone. A hydrogen fuel-cell system from Intelligent Energy powered the drone to stay in the air for approximately two hours.

The same drone remained airborne for twenty minutes when equipped with its standard lithium-ion battery. These fuel cells are also much faster to recharge. However, there are also disadvantages. The technology is expensive, and fuel-cell systems are heavier than batteries, which makes the drone less energy efficient. Fuel-cell power systems for drones remain in the research and development phase.

Most aircraft rely on combustion engines. This method generates significant force. "Using a high-energy-density energy source like gasoline, and converting it to electric power, and doing it efficiently, gives you the equivalent of a 'super battery,'" says Top Flight Technologies cofounder Long Phan.[10] He also adds, "The key is having an abundance of power and total energy. That's what . . . gasoline gives you."[11] This power allows drones to be larger or carry more weight than battery-powered models. Drones powered by gasoline or other fuels also offer longer and faster flights. There are significant downsides. The gas-powered drone is much louder. Also, these

DRONES, FIRST USE IN A MILITARY ROLE

During the First Lebanon War (1982–1985), Operation Mole Cricket 19 used small drones in a combat situation for the first time. Israeli forces used small drones called Scouts and Mastiffs as bait for the Syrian surface-to-air missiles. The Syrian forces turned on the radar systems for the missiles in order to shoot down the drones. Successfully tricking the Syrian surface-to-air missile systems allowed Israeli pilots to use bombs and missiles that home in on radio signals to take out the radar systems. As a result, Israeli pilots were safe. Drones were also used during the conflict to monitor airfields in order to report when Syrian planes took off. This strategy for drone use in combat has been used by Israeli forces many times since Operation Mole Cricket 19.

drones are inherently dangerous, as they fly unmanned with a full tank of flammable gas.

It is possible to have a constant power supply to a drone. This source of power is known as tethering. Tethering simply means having it plugged into a power supply cable during flight. This limits the distance of flight to the length of the cable.

The last method is called laser transmission. It involves beaming a laser from a station on the ground to a drone in flight. A device on the drone converts the laser's energy into useful electricity. This allows the UAV to stay in the air indefinitely. This is because when the power runs low, it can fly into range of the laser beam and receive a fresh supply of electricity. This process works similarly to solar power, except it is not dependent on the sun. Much like hydrogen-powered drones, cost and availability are limiting factors for this technology, as it is still experimental.

CONTROLLING THE FLIGHT

All of these devices need to be controlled by either human interaction or programmable computer software. The device that tells the drone what to do is called the controller. The controller must be able to communicate wirelessly with the drone in order for in-flight commands to take place.

Controllers typically communicate with drones through radio waves. Many consumer drone controllers utilize Wi-Fi. This uses radio waves to connect the controller and the drone. This capability allows smartphones and tablets to be used as controllers because those devices are designed to transmit and receive Wi-Fi signals.

A critical element to tracking the flight is an onboard GPS chip. A GPS chip receives signals from satellites orbiting the Earth.

By comparing the timing of signals from multiple satellites, the GPS chip can determine the drone's exact position on the planet. The drone's computer can use the GPS chip to log where takeoff occurred too. This is useful in the event the drone needs to find its own way back home. GPS is also a useful element for preprogrammed drone functions. A human controller can create a planned flight path based on GPS coordinates. Then the drone is instructed to fly to each of these points.

WORDS IN CONTEXT

horizon
The line where the sky and Earth's surface appear to meet.

In modern drones, there are small sensors that assist in proper flight control. One is the accelerometer. This sensor tells the operator exactly how the drone is accelerating from side to side. Another sensor is the gyroscope. This sensor tells the controller about the rotational direction of the drone. Much like in airplanes, a gyroscope is commonly used to determine the **horizon**. It is easy to determine the horizon while standing on the ground, but it can be difficult while airborne. These two sensors are often combined to create what is known as the onboard microelectromechanical systems (MEMS). These systems work with the drone's engine or engines to ensure the drone's flight is steady and level.

A computer system is a critical component, as it sends, receives, records, or changes signals between the UAV in the air and the controller on the ground. "If you lose signal link, you may have a limited ability to re-assert control over the aircraft," says Paul Scharre, director of the Future of Warfare Initiative at the Center for a New American Security.[12] Results can be catastrophic if a signal is disturbed or lost between the two. Having a reliable backup plan is essential. This is especially true in drones carrying out highly sensitive or dangerous missions. Backup plans might include returning to base using GPS from satellites or circling in the air at the last point of contact. For consumer drones this most often means flying back to the takeoff location.

ACCESSORIZING THE DRONE

All drones follow the principles of flight, require a power source, and need a method of control. Beyond these basic elements, drones can have a wide variety of features and functions. The versatility of drone technology is part of the reason it has exploded in popularity. Individuals, companies, and government agencies all have specific intentions when they decide to purchase a drone. Two of today's most common drone uses are imaging and transportation.

Imaging means the drone can transmit video to the operator. The ability of drones to fly and hover so freely has created a huge opportunity for photographers and videographers. Drones made for imaging implement the latest camera technology. They take breathtaking photos and videos. Sometimes two or more cameras are mounted to the UAV for additional imaging modes. Some drones, including those designed for racing, are often paired with first-person viewing (FPV) goggles. This lets the operator fly the drone from the view of the drone. This view is helpful when racing around corners and dodging obstacles.

Drone pilots can often control these cameras with smartphones, allowing the drones to fly and take pictures at the same time. Most consumer drones are able to record the video transmitted to the operator during flight. Transmitting video gives the operator the ability to see from the perspective of the drone. Many users purchase drones simply to enjoy this experience in real time. Mounting cameras on drones has also provided a safer way to photograph dangerous subjects. Photographer Joey Lawrence explains, "In the past, you'd have to ride in a helicopter, which is an extremely dangerous or expensive thing, in a war zone."[13]

THE DIVERSITY OF DRONES

There are many ways to classify drones, including by size, function, and power source. The most common and fundamental form of drone classification is how it flies. The three primary types of drones are multirotor, single-rotor, and fixed-wing.

Multirotor drones are the most common product in the public market. They use multiple downward-facing rotors—typically four, six, or eight—to generate lift like a helicopter. This type of UAV is usually simple for even beginners to fly. It hovers well, providing a steady airborne platform for photography. It can take off and land anywhere, instead of requiring a runway. The disadvantages of this type of UAV include its limited flight time, because it uses a lithium ion battery, and its inability to carry heavy loads.

Single-rotor drones closely resemble conventional helicopters in appearance and flight. With only one rotor, they are inherently less stable. These units are typically gas powered, which makes them more powerful, more expensive, and potentially more dangerous. Like multirotor drones, they have the ability to hover, but they require more training for the operator to become proficient.

Fixed-wing UAVs fly like standard airplanes. The use of wings to generate lift gives these drones longer ranges and faster speeds than their rotary-based counterparts. The downsides of these models are their need for a runway and their inability to hover. In addition, they are often difficult to fly. If a large fixed-wing drone cannot land on a

A DRONE'S-EYE VIEW

Virtual-reality (VR) goggles are increasingly popular gadgets. They allow the user to feel fully immersed in a computer-generated environment. The drone company DJI is applying this technology to real-time footage.

Released in 2017, the DJI Goggles allow customers to see live-streaming video from the perspective of their drone. The experience is so immersive it's similar to watching a 216-inch (549 cm) home-theater screen from 10 feet (3 m) away. The goggles allow the operator to move the drone's camera by turning his or her head. Users can also take pictures and video during flight. One mode allows the drone to fly itself while the viewer simply enjoys the sights. Beyond normal FPV functions, the goggles will "also allow you to control the camera—set focus, take pictures, or start and stop recording."

Quoted in "DJI's VR-Like Goggles Let You Control Your Drone Cam with Your Head," *PetaPixel*, April 25, 2017. petapixel.com.

runway, it will have to crash. This is particularly troublesome when used for military purposes.

The world of drone technology is constantly evolving. Businesses, militaries, and hobbyists are all finding new ways to use UAVs. The impact of these devices on society has the potential to be enormous. Microsoft cofounder Bill Gates predicts, "Drones will be more impactful than I think people recognize, in positive ways to help society."[14]

Chapter 2

Where Are Drones Found Today?

Drones have a wide variety of capabilities. Businesses and government agencies are putting these capabilities into practice. Drones used for personal recreation and enjoyment may be the most common in everyday life, but UAVs are playing a much larger role in society than many people might think.

DRONE DELIVERY SERVICE

Many people like to have personal items or food delivered directly to their residences. Rather than going out and searching for a product, it is much more convenient to purchase the product online. Many delivery services require multiple steps and drivers to get the goods to the final destination. Thanks to UAVs, waiting for an unpredictable delivery truck may soon become a thing of the past.

The online retail company Amazon is on the cusp of mainstreaming a drone-based delivery service called Prime Air. Multirotor and hybrid UAVs will bring packages weighing 5 pounds (2.2 kg) or less from a distribution center to the customer's address. The delivery process is completed in thirty minutes or less. The goal for the drones is for delivery to be fully autonomous, allowing the organization to become more efficient. Drones would plan routes, navigate obstacles, and return without human assistance. The hope is that drone delivery will be safer and faster than delivery trucks. The drone system could save Amazon significant money when compared to traditional delivery by saving on trucks, fuel, and payroll for a

With increases in automation, drones are currently being tested for deliveries by some companies. There are many factors that these companies have to take into account.

human driver. The limiting factor for such rapid delivery is weather. Amazon states it is only permitted to operate Prime Air during daylight hours and in clear weather conditions. However, research is being done to make it possible for UAVs to fly through harsher weather.

One of the most commonly delivered food items is pizza. Domino's Group CEO Don Meij believes, "Drone delivery will be an essential component of our pizza deliveries."[15] A New Zealand couple was the first recipient of airborne pizza. After the chicken pizzas were out of the oven, the drone delivered them to Emma and Johnny Norman in less than five minutes. Meij notes the benefits of using drones: "They can avoid traffic congestion and traffic lights, and safely reduce the delivery time and distance by travelling directly to customers' homes. This is the future."[16] The pizza company is looking to create more opportunities worldwide.

WORDS IN CONTEXT

regulation

A rule made and maintained by an authority.

There are roadblocks for companies looking to utilize drone technology for delivery. Start-up costs are a prohibitive factor for many businesses. Amazon is spending an estimated $150 million to launch the Prime Air program. More research and **regulation** must be in place to ensure public safety and security. There are already legal challenges to flying over private property. Currently, the FAA dictates private drones must not exceed 400 feet (122 m) in altitude or speeds of 100 miles per hour (161 km/h). But how high above private property a drone must stay in order to not infringe on the property is still unclear.

UAVs IN THE MEDIA

"We've spent the last 100 years taking images at ground level, so as soon as you change the perspective slightly, everything looks different, everything looks beautiful," says Romeo Durscher, the director of education at DJI and an avid aerial photographer.[17] Aerial photography is the practice of taking pictures from the sky. While manned aircraft have been used for aerial photography for more than a century, UAV technology has made it possible for anyone to try.

The movie industry has greatly benefited from drone technology. Some of the highest-grossing films of all time have included scenes shot using unmanned aircraft, including *Captain America: Civil War*, *Jurassic World*, and *Spectre*. The technology creates spectacular footage that would have been either too dangerous or impossible to acquire with previous technology.

Sports media outlets are also taking advantage of this new perspective. Fox Sports has used drones in its coverage of baseball, football, auto racing, and a variety of other sporting events. Senior Vice President, Technical and Field Operations Michael Davies says, "There are some shots that you simply can't get with conventional means."[18] He adds, "You can get a lot lower and close to different structures and ground elements with drones."[19] Broadcasters are phasing out less-effective helicopters and blimps, replacing them with drones for distant live shots of stadiums.

It isn't necessary to be a major organization to obtain incredible images. Many amateur and professional photographers use drones to take photographs and videos for special events. Football coaches use UAVs to film practices. Speaking about the advantage of drones over conventional video cameras, Idaho high-school football coach Paul Peterson states, "I think players get a much better feel for what they need to do and where they need to be on the field."[20] Multirotor drones are especially useful for indoor event photography because of their ability to hover.

DRONE RACING

Beyond the photography- and hobby-focused drones, there is also a growing market for drones built for speed. Online markets offer drones that are ready to race right out of the box or that must be built and programmed piece by piece. Some people will even purchase the frame, motors, transmitters, and other parts separately in order to build the fastest drone possible.

Local racing leagues have formed around the globe, allowing casual drone enthusiasts to test their skills and drones against others. Professional leagues have taken off as well. The Drone Racing League (DRL) has live-streamed races in arenas and has even partnered with ESPN. With racing-drone operators posting videos of acrobatic feats and clips of drones whizzing around obstacle courses to YouTube,

Racing drones have become incredibly popular. They are built for speed and agility.

interest in tricks and racing has exploded. The first season's races were aired on ESPN and Sky Sports across three continents in 2016. The season brought in 28.2 million views in the United States alone. Race teams took home prizes of up to $100,000.

Racing drones also use particular equipment suited for racing. Drone frames are made of carbon fiber to be as light and strong as possible. When these drones crash, it can be at speeds of up to 90 miles per hour (145 km/h). FPV goggles are preferred for racing over trying to race by line of sight. The goggles allow the operator to see the course as the drone flies through tunnels and hugs hairpin turns. This is the same view that the DRL uses for spectators. Camera feeds switch between drone cameras and cameras stationed at specific locations to show how the race develops.

REAL ESTATE SPECIALIST

In the competitive market of selling houses, real estate agents seek to gain any possible advantage to complete the sale. Drones offer a fresh perspective in the home buying and selling process. The CEO of real estate photography company VHT, Brian Balduf, explains, "In marketing real estate, you're trying to get people's attention and get them to spend more time looking at the property."[21]

One advantage is saving on the marketing budget. When aerial photography was expensive and required a helicopter, many realtors could not afford it. Often, aerial shots using a helicopter were reserved for houses selling for over a million dollars. Miami-based realtor Liza Mendez says, "As [drone imaging] becomes more affordable, I could see using this for just about any type of property."[22]

A prospective property buyer also gains helpful information with aerial images. Brian Balduf says, "You can fly out and give a tour of the entire estate."[23] They get a better sense of the yard and area around the house. The images also provide perspective of how the neighborhood looks, and some realtors provide an aerial tour of the community. This is particularly helpful for those unfamiliar with the area. Drone imagery is also used to evaluate the condition of the roof or other hard-to-reach features. A broader view of the entire property gives the buyer a much better picture before deciding to make a purchase.

The market for real estate drone use is rapidly expanding. As of 2017, the FAA reports 26 percent of all commercial drone flights are being used for real estate. There is debate among real estate agents about the technology. Many believe it is a gimmick, while other realtors are sold on the idea. If prices to use drone photography continue to fall, the practice is likely to become even more popular.

UTILITY COMPANIES INSPECTING WITH DRONES

Electric companies require massive **infrastructure** to maintain power to homes across the United States. In order to ensure a constant flow of electricity, inspections are done regularly on even the most dangerous structures. Like several other utility companies, Saint Louis–based Ameren has decided to replace humans with drones for these dangerous tasks.

> **WORDS IN CONTEXT**
>
> **infrastructure**
> Basic physical and organizational structures needed by society.

When discussing communications towers that are 200 feet (61 m) tall, Ameren's UAV technical lead, James Pierce, says, "With drones, we can quickly get the shots of the sites we need, which then gives us a full view of the conditions we're up against, and we can plan accordingly."[24] With millions of miles of electrical lines crisscrossing the country, often through remote locations, it is much faster to carry out inspections with UAVs than it is to send out crews. This strategy has allowed companies to catch problems before they happen by decreasing how long it takes to point out problem areas. Ameren project manager Robert Kennedy states, "Our whole goal with our drones is not having to react in the future."[25] Ameren wants to not have to react to new problems but to already be aware of these areas and fix them before a problem occurs.

Electric companies are not the only utility companies using UAV technology. Pipelines run across the US carrying oil and natural gas. Regularly monitoring these lines is crucial to preventing catastrophic leaks and environmental damage. It is estimated that oil and gas companies spend $37 billion a year to manually monitor and inspect pipelines. Drones are now being fitted with sensors to detect changes

TURNING ON THE LIGHTS

In 2017, Hurricane Maria dismantled the power grid in Puerto Rico. Power lines that brought electricity to mountainous rural areas were in ruins. The jungle terrain, which features ravines 1,000 feet (305 m) wide, made manual repair very difficult and time consuming. The power company Duke Energy turned to drone technology for a solution.

The company flew a drone carrying a lightweight nylon cord from pole to pole. Once the guide cord was in place at the next pole, workers attached and pulled the heavy electric line along the cord. After all the necessary lines were placed, power was restored. Thanks to help from these drones, 94 percent of Duke Energy's assigned area had power in a little over a month. This type of work is traditionally done using helicopters, but Duke Energy made the switch to drones.

in the integrity of the pipelines. The sensors detect rust or corrosion, which indicates a failure that requires immediate attention. As with power-line maintenance, drone technology is a much faster, safer, and more cost-effective strategy for inspecting pipelines.

INFRASTRUCTURE MAINTENANCE

The United States has more than 600,000 bridges. Nearly 40 percent of them are over fifty years old. In 2016, 9.1 percent of bridges were deemed to be structurally deficient by the American Road and Transportation Builders Association. Without proper inspection, monitoring, and repair, these structures are susceptible to catastrophic failure. With bridges getting older, it is necessary to find a solution to quickly and efficiently inspect these bridges before it is too late.

On August 2, 2007, a major freeway bridge on Interstate 35W in Minneapolis, Minnesota, collapsed. It was during rush hour with bumper-to-bumper traffic when the bridge gave way and plummeted into the Mississippi River. Thirteen people lost their lives, and many more were seriously injured. It was a tragic example of how infrastructure maintenance is vital for public safety.

Minnesota officials decided to make bridge safety a state priority. Inspections had to improve. State engineers now use the power of drones to ensure the safety of bridges. Beginning in 2015, Minnesota began using drones to scan entire bridges and evaluate hard-to-reach spots that often hide critical problems. The images are loaded into a software program. The software creates a three-dimensional model that shows engineers the trouble spots and deterioration rates of the bridges. This is a much more thorough and cost-effective strategy than crews inspecting bridges on foot with digital cameras. Some traditional pieces of inspection equipment cost well over $1 million each.

FARMERS TAKE FLIGHT

The farming industry has come a long way since the horse-pulled plow. Farmers have embraced new technology to improve the quantity and quality of their crops. Someday, there may be more drones working the fields than tractors.

On many farms, there is an enormous amount of land to monitor. Drones quickly cover this ground and perform checks on crops and livestock at speeds that are impossible by foot or tractor. One method that drones use to monitor the health of crops is time-lapse photography. If a drone passes over crops multiple times over the course of several days, reviewing the pictures shows whether the plants are thriving or wilting. This aerial inspection helps the farmer determine what course of treatment is necessary for the crops.

Drones are useful for tasks that can be dangerous for human workers. The Yamaha RMAX drone wastes less harmful pesticides while spraying crops.

Many farmers choose to spray crops with fertilizer and **pesticides**. This process can be dangerous for humans when the spraying is done by hand. Another technique for crop spraying is to use helicopters or small airplanes. These aircraft fly very low to the ground, often making low passes near power lines and roadways. Piloting them is considered one of the most dangerous jobs in the farming industry. The Yamaha RMAX was invented to eliminate these dangers. The RMAX is a single-rotor UAV equipped with tanks of pesticide or fertilizer. These drones have been shown to be more precise than tractors. This method cuts long-term costs and workers' potential exposure to hazardous chemicals.

WORDS IN CONTEXT

pesticides
Substances used to kill harmful organisms.

The uses available to businesses are only going to expand as technology improves and regulations reflect changes in safety and efficiency. Companies are looking to increase productivity in an effort to generate higher profits and create better products. The government has also found uses for UAVs. The primary achievements in government-run drone programs have been demonstrated in national defense and resource management.

EYE IN THE SKY

Government-owned drones are far more powerful and capable than anything that is purchased or operated for commercial or recreational use. Drones make up over 30 percent of all US military aircraft. The US military and intelligence agencies use UAVs to monitor strategic locations for reconnaissance and data collection.

Northrup Grumman is the defense contractor that invented and produces the Block 30 Global Hawk, a fixed-wing UAV. It flies at an incredible altitude of 60,000 feet (18,300 m), which is almost twice the height of commercial jets. The Global Hawk has the ability to fly up to thirty-two consecutive hours, capturing vital information and imagery that is sent directly to field commanders. This UAV uses state-of-the-art camera technology, including infrared sensors. This allows operators to view and distinguish between aircraft, vehicles, missiles, and people in real time and with precision. Each Global Hawk comes at a price of over $131 million. Considering the high cost and the sophisticated technology embedded in the drone, it is catastrophic to lose a drone of this caliber.

On the other end of the scale are mini-drones. Once thought to be merely a product of science fiction, these tiny devices have actually been on the battlefield for years. A Norwegian manufacturer, Prox Dynamics, created the drone known as Black Hornet. It measures a mere 4 inches (10 cm) long and 1 inch (2.5 cm) wide. This miniaturized single-rotor drone has been a lifesaver.

Many British soldiers carry the Black Hornet drone on their utility belts. Primarily used in Afghanistan, the mini-drone is deployed to safely look above walls and around corners. This handheld device is equipped with three cameras to give the soldier three views at a time. This information is used to determine whether and how to engage an enemy as well as to search for unknown hazards. While the cost is approximately $40,000 per Black Hornet, the safety it provides the soldier is priceless.

Some argue that drones are not worth the price tag. But if drones aren't doing the flying then humans are. The F-22 Raptor, which requires human pilots, comes in at $143 million per plane.

WAITRESS DRONES

In Singapore, the restaurant industry has a significant shortage of workers. Restaurants may soon employ drones to bridge the gap. These autonomous drones use infrared sensors strategically placed around the restaurant to deliver up to 4.4 pounds (2 kg) of food to waiters. The drones will "fly above human height before descending to a docking station, where waiters will take them to tables." The plan is to expected to increase the restaurant's productivity by 25 percent.

The goal is to free up human staff to perform more difficult tasks and interact with guests. This human-robotic relationship may improve the working and dining experience. Initially, these delivery drones could be more entertaining than financially practical. "It's going to be expensive and cumbersome," says drone-law attorney Jonathan Rupprecht. "But it's great marketing. I sort of want to go to the restaurant just to watch them."

Quoted in "Can't Hire Enough Waiters at Your Restaurant? Hire a Drone," ***MarketWatch*****, February 11, 2015. marketwatch.com.**

Two unmanned MQ-9 Reapers could be purchased with the same amount of money. A loss of a Reaper is steep, but it is far cheaper than a plane. It is also much safer. For budgeting purposes, increasing drone usage over manned aircraft for reconnaissance saves the military and taxpayers extraordinary sums of money in the long term. Keeping a watchful eye is only one military use for drone technology. Another well-documented drone delivers a deadly punch.

THE LETHAL SKIES

The General Atomics Predator drone forever changed the face of warfare. This remotely piloted aircraft was originally labeled model RQ-1 and was designed for surveillance use. The *R* is the Department of Defense (DOD) designation for reconnaissance. The letter *Q* stands for remotely piloted aircraft system. The *1* identifies the number in the series. In 2002, the Predator drone was modified to carry weapons and was subsequently renamed MQ-1. The *M* stands for multirole. The MQ-1 Predator performs reconnaissance and combat duties. Capable of flying at altitudes of 25,000 feet (7,600 m), the Predator is difficult for the enemy to detect.

The latest model of the weaponized drone is the MQ-9 Reaper. It flies much higher than the retired MQ-1 Predator, reaching altitudes of up to 50,000 feet (15,200 m). This aircraft has a range of 1,150 miles (1,850 km) and cruises at 230 miles per hour (370 km/h), making it much more difficult than the Predator to target. Another benefit of the Reaper is that it has better cameras and sensors for acquiring intelligence and reconnaissance during flight than the Predator. The updated technology makes it more efficient, as it can accomplish multiple missions on the same flight.

The Reapers are particularly lethal due to the missiles they carry. A standard Reaper is equipped with four Hellfire missiles. Once the pilot selects the target, a laser-guided pathway is established. This pathway guides the missile to swiftly and accurately hit the target. Combining military drones with these missiles is a stealthy and deadly combination. The enemy is often not able to see the drone because of altitude. The Hellfire missile travels at **supersonic** speeds, so it reaches its destination before it can be heard. These missiles can be loaded with various types of explosives.

It is important for the operators to determine the type of explosion to be used. Too little explosive power, and the missile may not be effective. Too much can lead to unintended civilian casualties around the target. This particularly concerns those worried about drone usage. Modern combat often occurs in densely populated areas, and the targets of recent drone strikes have been known to use civilians as a form of human shields. Drone strikes are authorized by high-level commanders, and sometimes the president even makes the final decision about whether to launch a strike.

> **WORDS IN CONTEXT**
>
> **supersonic**
> Faster than the speed of sound.

While highly controversial, drone strikes have proven effective in modern warfare. They have been used to kill high-value terrorist targets. Being able to remotely strike a well-guarded enemy is a critical component in saving lives of military personnel. After terrorist leader Osama bin Laden's 2011 death, letters were recovered between him and his deputies that showed the effectiveness of drones in limiting the movement of his organization. One letter wrote, "Reduce the work, meaning stopping many of the operations so we can move around less, and be less exposed to strikes."[26] Clearly, Predator and Reaper drones give terrorist leaders something to think about.

Supporters of the drone program argue that some collateral damage is an unfortunate but necessary reality of protecting the citizens at home. By targeting individuals and groups of terrorists, successful strikes disrupt coordination and leadership. Targeted strikes are thought to have prevented attacks on American and European soil. Supporters of drones argue that the world would be a far more dangerous place if not for these remote-controlled soldiers.

WILDLIFE AND NATURAL RESOURCES

Not all government-used UAV technology is applied toward the military. Drones equipped with cameras are used by government agencies to monitor wildlife and natural resources. Some devices are used by officials in the National Park and Forest Services.

Biologists use drones for counting and observing wildlife. Conducting wildlife surveys is critical, but it can be very expensive and sometimes dangerous using standard aircraft. When talking about drone usage for wildlife observation, wildlife biology professor David Bird of Montreal's McGill University states, "Drones can offer a very safe, green, and inexpensive alternative to manned aircraft."[27] Drones provide better image quality than traditional methods. They can be fitted with thermal cameras that provide even more information. And by using drones, natural resource officers are better equipped to photograph and apprehend **poachers**. Other benefits include being able to access dangerous or unreachable territory and possibly disturbing animals less than conventional aircraft.

Fighting and monitoring fires is a difficult and incredibly dangerous operation. During heavy fire seasons, there is often a shortage of manned aircraft. Thanks to innovations in UAV technology, unmanned devices are being deployed to help develop strategies before firefighters engage. The ScanEagle drone is the chief UAV utilized by the US government for firefighting. This fixed-wing craft is well suited for capturing information regarding the fire's size and behavior. Drones are flown much closer to the fires than manned aircraft, since there is no potential danger to a human pilot. The infrared camera attached to the ScanEagle shows firefighters where the hottest points of the wildfire are. This information helps allocate resources better and direct personnel to the areas of highest concern.

> **WORDS IN CONTEXT**
>
> **poachers**
>
> A person who hunts or takes wild animals illegally.

While acquiring aerial images or video of these magnificent lands is tempting, it is important for individuals to understand and follow federal regulations for flying UAVs in national parks or national forests. In most cases, it is strictly illegal, except when issued a special permit. There have been instances of illegal drone activity disturbing the land and wildlife in these areas. Personal use of UAVs also poses a flight risk to official-use aircraft, including those used for firefighting.

Drone technology has shown a lot of promise for both the private and public sectors. It has the capability to take and save lives. Drones deliver pizzas and fight fires. The possibilities for UAVs are increasing every year. No matter who has their hands on drone technology, it is important that these vehicles be used responsibly. With decreasing cost and increased production, more and more people are flying drones. As with the spread of any new technology, this may lead to unintended consequences or dangerous situations.

Chapter 3

What Are the Risks and Drawbacks of Drones?

Just as with any new field, there have been questions and concerns about the expansion of drone technology. Some questions have even involved the overall well-being of society. There have been troubling incidents involving UAVs that have made national news. Transportation safety, privacy concerns, terrorism threats, and societal consequences must all be carefully examined when writing and enforcing regulations for a new and growing field. Drone technology is expected to be very helpful to society, but at the same time it carries the potential to be very destructive.

THE UNFRIENDLY SKIES

According to the FAA, the agency handled over 15 million flights during 2016 in the United States. The FAA's Air Traffic Organization helped more than 43,000 flights per day. During peak times, there are an average of 5,000 commercial aircraft in the sky. These planes carry over 2.5 million passengers per day. That is a lot of traffic in the sky.

Drones can potentially create complications for airborne traffic. In Quebec City, Canada, on October 12th, 2017, the first reported drone and commercial airplane collision occurred. As the passenger plane began its descent to land, the pilots briefly saw something that immediately hit the plane's left wing. Canadian Transport Minister Marc Garneau declared, "This should not have happened, that drone

The FAA tracks and organizes all flight traffic in America. Adding drones that may not be following regulations can make for dangerous situations.

should not have been there, and it's important to point out that the aircraft are particularly vulnerable when they're on final approach."[28] Many experts believe it won't be the last collision. While the plane landed safely, future crews and passengers might not be so lucky if involved in a midair collision.

Earlier in 2017, on September 21, a US Army Black Hawk helicopter was struck by a drone flying at an altitude of 500 feet (150 m). "One blade was damaged, dented in two spots and requires replacement," noted Army Lieutenant Colonel Joe Buccino.[29] Fortunately, there were no injuries or fatalities.

ILLEGAL DRONE STRIKES?

In modern warfare against terrorist groups and individuals, conventional methods are often disregarded by both sides. One highly controversial drone strike was on an American citizen, Anwar al-Awlaki. On September 30, 2011, al-Awlaki was targeted and killed in Yemen, marking the first time an American citizen had been executed by his own government without a trial since the Civil War. Anwar al-Awlaki was certainly not any ordinary US citizen. He was a recognized leader of the terrorist group Al-Qaeda in Yemen.

President Barack Obama justified the strike by stating, "I will not hesitate to use force to protect our nation, including from the threat of terrorism." While most critics do not necessarily mourn the death of a terrorist leader, they believe it sets a dangerous precedent. If a president decides to authorize the killing of an American citizen without trial, what legally stops a future president from doing the same for any reason?

Quoted in "The Lessons of Anwar al-Awlaki," ***New York Times*****, August 27, 2015. nytimes.com.**

Both instances violated regulations. Both drones were flying above the altitude limit of 400 feet (122 m). Investigators also believe the drone pilots were violating line-of-sight regulations, which dictate the operator must be able to see the drone in the sky throughout the duration of the flight. In both collisions, the pilot of the drone was never discovered. Unfortunately, no matter how strict regulations are, there are always those who either are uninformed or choose to intentionally break the law.

DANGER ON THE GROUND

The sky is not the only place where accidents with drones have occurred. Whether through device malfunction, improper training, or recklessness, accidental collisions have already happened between consumer drones and people on the ground. Many of the victims had no idea there was a drone flying over them before the accident. Some victims even have been knocked unconscious.

On the German Autobahn there is no enforced speed limit. Many drivers push their vehicles to the limit. If there is a collision, most expect it to be between cars. In 2015, a man was driving on the freeway when a drone, 16 inches (40 cm) wide, crashed into the windshield of his car. Given the speed at which drones and cars travel, it is incredible the driver was not seriously injured or killed.

Towers, homes, and other buildings are also at risk of drone collisions. Two iconic American structures have been accidentally hit by drones. In 2016, a man accidentally flew his drone into the fortieth floor of the Empire State Building in Manhattan in New York City. In the same year, another drone operator crashed his UAV into the Space Needle in Seattle, Washington. Fortunately, no one was hurt in either instance, but both drone operators were criminally charged.

Another man in Seattle was sentenced to thirty days in jail after his photography drone crashed into a crowd of people, knocking one person unconscious. While Seattle Municipal Court Judge Willie Gregory didn't believe the act was intentional, he ruled that the operator "engaged in conduct that put people in danger of being injured."[30] This is not the only instance of individuals being injured by drone collisions. There are many cases of unintended human–drone contact.

BEWARE OF THE BLADES

Although drones are fun to operate, they can potentially cause injury if operated by reckless individuals. The drone operator certainly needs to put the safety of others first but also cannot forget their own personal well-being. On single-rotor, multirotor, or fixed-wing UAVs, the

WORDS IN CONTEXT

apparatus
Technical equipment needed for a particular activity or purpose.

spinning blades are an especially hazardous **apparatus** for hands and fingers.

The Cleveland Indians star pitcher Trevor Bauer was on the team that participated in the 2016 World Series. Days before the American League Championship Series, perhaps the biggest game of his career, Bauer had to make a visit to the emergency room. While tinkering with his custom-built drone, a propeller caused a serious cut to his right pinky finger. Trevor Bauer pitches right-handed. He made an attempt to play in the game but was taken out after only twenty-one pitches due to the cut reopening. The team went on to win the game, and Bauer continues to work on and fly his fleet of drones.

BAD NEIGHBORS

Nosy neighbors can be annoying. With drones buzzing around recreationally and commercially, drones may invade personal privacy. With UAVs used frequently for real estate and recreation, seeing these devices is not uncommon in residential areas. While most just go about their business, other pilots use drones for improper reasons.

There has been an outbreak of cases in which individuals have used drones to spy on unsuspecting people. A woman in southern Australia had a frightening incident during the night. She was sleeping alone when an object, which turned out to be a drone, repeatedly ran into her window. The unnamed victim told the local news outlet, "I feel violated, feel it's intrusive and feel scared, intimidated."[31] Another victim in a similar incident shared this fear, stating, "It's got to the point where I now sleep with a large wooden bat in my bed."[32] The drone pilot was never caught.

While drones have been used by law enforcement to catch lawbreakers, criminals also use UAVs for illicit purposes. Burglars use drones to make their plans. Drones with cameras are used to assess potential entry, exit, and weak points in security. There is a gang that has committed burglaries in New York, New Jersey, Pennsylvania, Illinois, Minnesota, and Missouri using drones to facilitate its crimes.

It is important that people stay vigilant about unusual drone activity. "If members of the public observe drones being used in areas which make them suspicious they should contact police," urges Paul Ford, secretary of the Police Federation National Detectives Forum.[33] He adds, "At the end of the day this is a reminder to householders to make sure their homes are secure."[34]

FOREIGN SPY IN THE SKY

A memo from the Los Angeles office of the Immigration and Customs Enforcement (ICE) bureau asserts Chinese company DJI's drones are "providing U.S. critical infrastructure and law enforcement data to the Chinese government."[35] DJI is responsible for creating some of the most popular drones in the marketplace. The Phantom and Mavic series drones are flying over the United States. While these drones are enjoyable and functional for many owners, US law-enforcement officials are concerned.

DJI responded to the memo stating, "The allegations in the bulletin are so profoundly wrong as a factual matter that ICE should consider withdrawing it, or at least correcting its unsupportable assertions."[36] However, ICE has claimed with "moderate confidence" that the accusations are true, based upon a source in the industry "with first and secondhand access."[37] The US Army and Australian Defense Force directed their members to cease using DJI drones. The claims are still being investigated by the US Department of Homeland Security (DHS).

The DHS believes that DJI is intentionally sending collected data to the Chinese government and military. The DHS states this allows the Chinese government to "coordinate physical or cyber attacks against critical sites" in the United States.[38] According to the DHS report, the drones have advanced GPS and facial-recognition software that is still functional even when the device is powered off. Cloud-based servers from the company also house such information as users' phone, email, video, and picture data. Even if the spying claims turn out to be incorrect, this type of data collection does hold the potential for abuse.

Nations have spied on each other for decades, and in some cases centuries. They are always trying to gain military or economic advantages over one another. Although information may not be immediately used to cause harm, sensitive data must be highly secured. Drone technology for spying has possible harmful effects, and UAVs could be used by groups that mean harm to others.

CYBER THREAT

Drones, just like phones and computers, can be accessed remotely. It is one of the biggest safety concerns surrounding drones. If hackers gain control of a drone, they can fly the drone and use the camera and GPS technology to gather information about the owner or even harass him or her.

Companies have written software to protect drones from hacking. Not all drones have antihacking software or features, but it is incredibly important to have for drones in certain industries. A hacker could do far more damage gaining access to a military-grade Reaper or a drone that belongs to a natural-gas company than just invade

Drones are not immune to cyberattacks. Drones can even be used for spying and digital attacks.

someone's privacy. Larger threats have to be taken into account when thinking about the security and future of drones.

FLYING TERROR

Drone delivery has pushed the industry to increase the carrying capacity of UAVs. But drones that can carry a larger mail-order package can also carry a larger dangerous load, such as explosives. Law-enforcement officials are concerned that such a delivery may happen soon.

"I think we do know that terrorist organizations have an interest in using drones," says FBI director Christopher Wray, who adds, "I think that the expectation is that it is coming here, imminently."[39]

Federal officials seem to believe a terrorist attack using a drone is a matter of when, not if. The director of the National Counterterrorism Center, Nicholas Rasmussen, believes organizations such as the Islamic State in Iraq and Syria (ISIS) have already used drones in overseas attacks.

In 2011, a UAV attack on American soil nearly happened. A Massachusetts physics graduate was arrested for planning to use three GPS-guided aircraft rigged with explosives to bomb the Pentagon and US Capitol buildings. The plot was foiled by FBI agents, but officials fear similar plans are in the works.

The FAA and other government officials are concerned by the possibility of drone operators intentionally crashing their UAVs into commercial airliners, which could lead to a devastating crash. "Terrorists continue to target commercial aviation and air cargo," reads a bulletin from the DHS.[40] The hard components of a drone, including the motor and the battery, are especially damaging to a jet engine.

Basic drones are very easy to purchase. If a terrorist wants to harm people, drones can be adapted to create a flying device with extremely deadly potential. Drones are not limited by fences or walls, leading many to worry about potential attacks on outdoor stadium events or large public gatherings. Federal government and local law-enforcement agencies have been testing systems to track commercial drones. One such attempt to track a drone was used on New Year's Eve 2014 in the busy Times Square celebration.

Another potential danger is that terrorists could use drones like the Yamaha RMAX used by farmers. The Yamaha RMAX is prefitted with large liquid-holding tanks. While the approved use is for fertilizing and helping crops, officials fear using even basic chemicals could lead to catastrophic chemical attacks. "Even gasoline spread as a vapour when ignited has 15 times the explosive energy of the equivalent weight of TNT," says Professor David Hastings Dunn of the University of Birmingham in the United Kingdom.[41] He also writes, "A drone attack would be psychologically unnerving and terror inducing."[42]

> **WORDS IN CONTEXT**
>
> **rogue**
> Operating outside normal or desirable controls.

There are many obstacles and challenges to face when trying to combat **rogue** drones. Increases in flight regulation and stricter permitting processes are coming, but changes in laws will only help prevent accidents. Currently illegal for public use, drone-tracking equipment developed by Black Sage Technologies is being researched and tested to stop rogue drones. The equipment works by identifying a drone with Doppler radar, visualizing it with a high-definition camera, and finally disabling the drone with radio waves that jam and paralyze the UAV. The FAA must first be convinced the equipment is safe to deploy before it is cleared for widespread law enforcement use.

JOB-KILLERS

Drones, robots, and other forms of automation cut costs for many businesses. For millions of American workers, those cost savings are actually their salaries. Economists predict that nearly 50 percent of all jobs will be replaced by automation by the 2030s. Drones play a large role in this workplace evolution.

Auditing and accounting firm PricewaterhouseCoopers (PwC) published a report that suggests drones have the potential to replace $127 billion in human labor. The infrastructure and agriculture industries are making the largest savings, combining to gain over $77 billion with use of drone technology. Drone deliveries may eventually make the delivery driver obsolete. Many pilots, soldiers, and even lifeguards have had their jobs replaced or changed by UAVs.

Business Insider writer Chris Weller notes, "In fact, any job that relies on human vision and judgement, specifically from hard-to-reach vantage points, will likely have to confront the possibility of drones in the future."[43] However, there are new career opportunities in drone technology and services. One example involves becoming a drone operator for the job being replaced. The replaced worker is knowledgeable about the decision-making for that job, so he or she might be the person best suited to control the drone doing the tasks. However, the overall loss of so many jobs is an economic problem in the making.

WORDS IN CONTEXT

philanthropy
The practice of giving to help make life better for other people.

When so many jobs are eliminated, a lot of strain is placed on society. Some individuals who lose their positions need to be retrained into another field. This often requires funding from personal savings, government spending, loans, or **philanthropy**. The resulting impact is a loss of other spending into the market, which slows the national and global economy. But as growing markets are flooded with newly trained workers, spending and the economy will grow. A concerning issue is that many retraining programs are not advancing as quickly as the technology. The world may not yet be ready for such a profound change in technology-based jobs.

DISRUPTING NATURE

Humans are quite curious, especially when it comes to nature and animals. Drones are allowing people to get closer to wildlife, but this new view is actually hazardous to the very subjects of interest.

"The drones can get really close, and I'm sure the footage might be fantastic, but they're disturbing the eagles," said Eagle Watch organizer Wolfgang Pauli.[44] Co-organizer Judith Knapp notes, "We need to protect them. If they're flying around, get scared, if they're nervous about a drone, they could hurt themselves with terrible consequences."[45] Drone operators caught violating regulations are fined for disturbing wildlife at the discretion of a conservation officer. For some that is not enough of a deterrent.

Birds are not the only animals that can come to harm because of UAVs. Marine animals such as seals and sea lions get nervous when flying invaders get close. Drones can cause stress in the animals, which leads to behavioral changes, including the inability to feed or rest. The animals may also hurt or abandon their young because of drone harassment. Even whales are affected by drone use. Whales have been seen turning over to get a better view of nearby UAVs. Despite regulation passed in 1972, the Marine Mammal Protection Act that protects marine mammals from harassment, people still feel getting pictures is more important than the health and well-being of these creatures.

Animals are not always predictable, and drones lead to further unpredictability. In Wyoming, a man was issued a $280 ticket after his drone triggered a herd of 1,500 elk to stampede over one-half mile (805 m). The herd was resting in a refuge valley in western Wyoming when the operator launched the drone at them. The winter had already caused great stress in the animals. The drone harassment could harm to the herd's chances of survival.

Respecting nature is critical to its health and future. Drone operators must be very careful of their surroundings and consider the potential impact that even the smallest of UAVs might have on wildlife.

Drones have been used for surveillance and trespassing. It is important to be aware of suspicious activity.

NEIGHBORHOOD DRONE BATTLES

While operating a drone is fun and exciting, not everyone shares that opinion. Many people strongly dislike any drone activity, especially when it encroaches on them or their property. While some irritated individuals contact law enforcement, others take matters into their own hands.

Kentucky neighbors William Merideth and David Boggs had a very public dispute about Boggs's drone use. The drone was being flown over Merideth's property, which Merideth didn't like. Using property defense as his argument, he grabbed a gun to shoot the drone out of the sky. "I had no way of knowing (if) it was a predator looking at my children," insists Merideth.[46]

After the drone was shot down, the two men confronted one another. The incident quickly escalated. After Boggs asked Merideth to replace the drone, Merideth pointed the gun at Boggs. Police officers were quickly dispatched to the scene, where Merideth was subsequently arrested and charged with first-degree endangerment for shooting into the air and criminal mischief. The charges were later dismissed in court.

It is easy to see how tensions rise considering how drone use has been shown to be both good and bad. Property rights are a consideration for anyone wishing to fly a UAV. There are several examples of heated exchanges over flight paths and perceived reckless drone use. People on the ground may fear drones are spying on them or taking unauthorized pictures. A responsible drone pilot always follows federal law and local regulations, as irresponsible behavior makes it more difficult for everyone to enjoy or utilize a drone. A good practice is to always be courteous while operating a drone, including informing neighbors of a flight prior to use.

There are significant safety, ethical, economic, and environmental hurdles that must be addressed as drones find their fullest potential. While drones push society further and further toward the future, the public must be convinced that the benefits outweigh the risks. The world will be a very different place if all of the possible applications of drones come true. It is up to researchers, engineers, and society as a whole to determine the role of drones.

Chapter 4

What Is the Future of Drones?

Drone technology holds the possibility to change the trajectory of society. While current UAVs have already demonstrated amazing capabilities, there are still many more in research and development. Society must decide that drones will do more good than harm for the technology to reach its full potential. If modern civilization chooses to embrace drone technology, UAVs will play an even larger role in many sectors, assisting in business, government, and everyday personal use.

SAFER FORM OF DELIVERY

Safety is a critical component of successful drone delivery. Health hazards and accidents are reasons many fear the universal use of the UAVs for product delivery. Safer and more portable drones are necessary. The École Polytechnique Fédérale de Lausanne (EPFL), a university in Switzerland, is close to solving these problems.

Researchers at the EPFL have designed a drone with an **origami**-inspired shell that encompasses the whole object. This design protects people and objects from the propellers and is designed to hold cargo for deliveries. This cage allows the drone to safely bounce off obstacles.

There are other benefits to this cage-style drone. The drone is designed to fold down to 8 percent of its flying size. In this configuration, it is easily stowed. It is small enough to fit in a backpack when not in use. The drone is also built with the ability to autonomously fly back to the sender. This is an essential feature for companies that want to use delivery drones.

> **WORDS IN CONTEXT**
>
> **origami**
> Japanese art of folding paper into figures and shapes.

In a research paper from the EPFL, project investigators stated they believe their proposed design can be scaled to "fly 2 kg [2 pounds] over 15 km [9 miles], which would cover 86 percent of the deliveries made by Amazon."[47] While the proposed weight limit is appropriate for most deliveries, it is not the only consideration. The size of the delivery is also important for this design because it must fit within the cage, no matter what it weighs.

The EPFL is also planning to design other safety-conscious drone models. The strategy is to design different drone types to be able to carry a variety of shapes and sizes of parcels. Additional cameras and safety parachutes are also being considered in case of emergency. Organizations and individuals have a lot to lose if the package cannot successfully be delivered. This is especially true for the future of transferring precious medical cargo.

MEDICAL DELIVERY DRONES

In the world of medicine, two of the most important factors for success are speed and accuracy. When a life is on the line, emergency and operating rooms often require blood or medical specimens. Large cities with multiple medical centers quickly deliver items between facilities. Rural or remote communities experience a significant delay in receiving lifesaving materials. Drone technology is being designed to increase the quality and pace of medical delivery.

Traditional methods of medical delivery involve having to navigate traffic and use roads. Drones could potentially save lives by making important deliveries much more quickly.

Drones have already been used to provide help for victims of disaster. Following a 2012 earthquake in Haiti, drones brought basic medical supplies and care packages to those in need.

More lives could be saved if rare types of blood could be delivered on demand. Dr. Cornelius A. Thiels of Mayo Clinic explains, "Blood is unique, because it's expensive and expires—platelets and thawed plasma last just five days—and the supply is very limited."[48] He believes drone technology can replace more expensive and time-consuming road-based courier services. In 2017, researchers from Johns Hopkins demonstrated that drones could safely deliver blood samples through the harsh Arizona desert. During the three-hour flight, the blood samples safely traveled 161 miles (259 km). The samples that flew arrived at a temperature of 76.6 degrees

Fahrenheit (25°C) while simultaneously driven samples recorded 81.1 degrees (27°C). The samples were tested, and the drone-delivered samples were considered superior. The driven samples began to degrade slightly as a result of increasing temperature. Project researcher Timothy Amukele states, "We expect that in many cases, drone transport will be the quickest, safest, and most efficient option to deliver some biological samples to a laboratory from rural or urban settings."[49] This example demonstrates a drone's potential utility in time-sensitive cases in rural communities.

Organ transplant is a highly sensitive medical procedure. Current technology requires organs to be delivered over the road from one facility to another. Several factors, including traffic and road conditions, can delay or cause the procedure to fail. Engineers are developing drones that are used to quickly and safely deliver human organs. There is also speculation that the technology will someday pair with bioengineering companies that create human-compatible pig-based organs. Delivering successful lab-created organs on demand by drones could revolutionize the medical field. According to the United Network for Organ Sharing, nearly twenty people die each day waiting for a transplant.

The CEO of Lung Biotechnology, Martine Rothblatt, believes a future drone system called the Manufactured Organ Transport Helicopter (MOTH) will bring down the number of deaths from people waiting for organs. She stated, "We anticipate delivering hundreds of organs a day, which means that the MOTH system will help save not only tens of thousands of lives but also millions of gallons of aviation transport gasoline annually."[50] The futuristic MOTH is a fully autonomous drone created by the Chinese company Ehang. It is modeled after the Ehang 184 drone, which was originally designed to carry human passengers.

ROBOTIC POLLINATORS

Bees are necessary for flowers to grow. Through pollination, bees transfer pollen from one plant to another. Pollen is the key ingredient that allows plants to reproduce. In 2016, the United States lost over 40 percent of all honeybee colonies. If the bee population steadily dwindles, crop growers across the world may struggle to produce food for humans, in addition to the loss of wildflowers that rely on bee pollination. While natural organisms like honeybees are the preferred pollinator, drones could soon help pollinate while the bee population rebounds.

The animal kingdom has led to innovations in technology. Airplanes, helicopters, and drones are no exception. Researcher Eijiro Miyako at the National Institute of Advanced Industrial Science and Technology in Japan has developed an insect-sized drone that mimics how bees transfer pollen. This new model of drone is coated with horse hair and a liquid gel. The drones are able to fly from flower to flower and collect and deposit pollen with this coating, but maneuvering the drones so precisely is incredibly hard.

> **WORDS IN CONTEXT**
> **entomologist**
> An expert of studying insects.

While tests have shown the method to be effective, there are still major roadblocks. To pollinate large areas of flowers and trees requires a huge fleet of pollinators. It takes an incredible number of robots to fully replace bees. University of Minnesota **entomologist** Marla Spivak says, "Two million colonies of bees are trucked in to pollinate the [California] almonds, and each colony has between ten and twenty thousand foragers."[51]

Bees are vital for pollinating plants. Robotic bees are being developed to help do this job.

Spivak also notes there are nearly 20,000 unique species of bees. Each has different abilities and characteristics that allow for pollination of the broad diversity of plants. Many types of drones would need to be designed. Spivak believes that current uses of pesticide-spraying drones could help decrease overall bee deaths. While no UAV may ever fully replace bees, drones can provide relief while scientists work to help the natural population rebound.

PEREGRINE POWER

There is another winged creature playing a role in helping communities. As individuals, gangs, and terrorist organizations begin to use drones to commit crimes, authorities are evolving to stay a step ahead. Another example of animal-influenced drone technology is used for defense. Futuristic drone technology is being inspired by one of the greatest aerial hunters, the peregrine falcon. This bird has the capability of striking prey in midair. Some predatory birds are actually being trained to take down drones. The peregrine falcon stalks airborne prey from high altitudes before diving and driving prey to the ground, reaching speeds near 200 miles per hour (322 km/h).

Professor Graham Taylor of the Oxford Zoology Department Flight Group said, "Our GPS tracks and on-board videos show how peregrine falcons intercept moving targets that don't want to be caught."[52] He adds, "Our next step is to apply this research to designing a new kind of visually guided drone, able to remove rogue drones safely from the vicinity of airports, prisons and other no-fly zones."[53] He compares their motions and attack mechanisms to visually guided missiles, noting, "Falcons are classic aerial predators, synonymous with agility and speed."[54]

WORDS IN CONTEXT

contraband
Goods that have been moved illegally.

Drones have been used for nefarious purposes, such as flying **contraband** like cell phones, drugs, and weapons into prisons. UAVs are also routinely encroaching into no-fly zones near sensitive sites and aircraft. When a rogue drone is identified, it is important for authorities to take it out. Researchers at Oxford University are closely studying the falcon's incredible capabilities to design a drone hunter. The research team was able to get a bird's-eye view of how the falcon closes in on the target. Miniature cameras and GPS trackers were placed on the bird. When released by a falconer, the bird attacked dummy targets that were towed by a drone.

The peregrine falcon is not the first bird to inspire to the future of flight. Speed, strength, and maneuverability are all being considered for defense purposes. However, it is another characteristic of birds that may be the most groundbreaking.

STRENGTH IN NUMBERS

Birds and flying insects often fly in patterns called flocks or swarms. When flying as a team, the individuals fly more efficiently. Grouping also provides safety. It is this tactic that the US Defense Advanced Research Projects Agency (DARPA) looks to unleash with UAVs.

The goal of the project is for a large aircraft to be able to deploy several small drones called Gremlins. The Gremlins would be a disruptive team flying together, capturing intelligence, performing coordinated attacks, and surveilling areas. While one UAV is useful to the military, a swarm of drones unlocks a new era of aviation defense technology. DARPA hopes the swarms of Gremlins will be able to overwhelm enemy defenses by sheer volume of aerial attackers.

The Gremlins are being designed to be recaptured by the aircraft that released them. Once secured, they are safely flown back home, where mechanics on the ground perform maintenance. DARPA expects the small UAVs to be ready to fly again within twenty-four hours of previous use. Each Gremlin has a life expectancy of approximately twenty uses. In terms of durability, this puts the technology between missiles and conventional aircraft.

Not only do the swarms promise more power and capability, they also decrease long-term aerial defense costs. The first airplane to deliver the swarm will be the Lockheed Martin C-130 transport aircraft. While this delivery aircraft is piloted by a human, future delivery and recovery planes could be UAVs. Someday there could be flocks of drones that in turn release smaller swarms.

Ehang and other companies are exploring automated flight. This could open up a way to commute without road traffic.

The power potential of the flock may soon be fully understood. The DOD has flown its own drone swarm. The DOD's small Perdix drones were designed to jam communications and provide surveillance. They have the ability to self-heal and demonstrate collective decision-making. This artificial-intelligence capability allows the drones to rearrange themselves if one or more were to fall out of the sky, similar to how birds fly in a flock.

THE FLYING CAR

Beginning several decades ago, many believed the future would be defined by the flying car. Visions of drivers and families leaving the home and taking to the skies from the garage have only existed in science fiction. Making personal flight realistic for society without extensive training always seemed out of reach. Thanks to advancement in UAV technology, the future is now on the verge of reality.

In 2016, Ehang made a bold promise at the Consumer Electronics Show in Las Vegas, Nevada. The organization pledged to build a fully autonomous drone capable of carrying passengers. Over 1,000 test flights later, the Ehang 184 is ready for takeoff. The supersized quadcopter has been demonstrated to carry up to 500 pounds (230 kg), climb 980 feet (300 m) vertically, withstand gale-force winds, and reach speeds just over 80 miles per hour (129 km/h). Ehang's CEO stated, "Now that we've successfully tested the Ehang 184, I'm really excited to see what the future holds for us in terms of air mobility."[55]

There are still many skeptics, despite what the company has boasted regarding testing. In February 2018, the company released footage of some of its testing. The video shows the 184 successfully taking off, flying, and landing with several different passengers onboard. This model of drone is completely electric, and it is capable of carrying a single passenger for just over twenty minutes of flight. The passenger simply inputs the destination of choice, and the drone creates an automated flight path. If any trouble arises, a present human pilot is able to take over the controls. Ehang is developing future models that will accommodate two passengers and also allow manual flight control of the aircraft if desired. Owners will be able to choose between conventional manual flight and simply being a passenger.

Ehang believes the first use will be for luxury rides because initial costs are projected to be high. However, the company wishes to make its drones available for the everyone. The company is working with officials in the city of Dubai in the United Arab Emirates to create a flying taxi service to help ease the city's congested streets.

The company believes prices of these passenger drones will come down when flight paths become better established and the need for a backup pilot is eliminated. While the dream of a flying car in every garage is not here yet, organizations like Ehang, Boeing, Bell, and NASA are close to bringing that idea to life.

The ride-sharing service company Uber is also getting into the drone taxi industry. The company's goal is to create a network of flying electric vehicles that take off and land vertically. Uber insists the vehicles are quieter and more cost effective than helicopters. In 2018, CEO Dara Khosrowshahi predicted the aircraft service testing in Los Angeles, California, by 2020.

PERSONAL SECURITY DRONES

Home security systems have been in place for many years. Many of them require extensive wiring and communication hardware installed into the house. The companies that provide these systems often charge monthly fees for services, and most do not offer video surveillance as a standard option. While some people and companies choose to put security cameras into their property, current models are fixed to a single location. This requires purchasing more expensive equipment. A few large companies and small start-ups are adapting drones to transform home security. The mobility of a single drone allows it to replace several cameras.

One company called Sunflower Labs is creating a hybrid system. It is developing prototypes that combine stationary sensors with drones. The sensors are able to directly communicate with the drone. A multirotor drone is equipped with cameras that stream a live video feed to the owner. Therefore, if any motion or activity is detected, the drone can fly quickly to capture footage anywhere on the property. This technology could change the home security industry.

Drones are being integrated into some home security systems. Their ability to hover and fly makes them more valuable than a normal camera.

There are still hurdles to clear for this system to be practical. The drone must be able to steer clear of obstacles, especially humans and pets. If the multirotor design is the model of choice, indoors or outdoors the blades could cause serious damage during a collision. Another concern is the threat of a cybersecurity breach. Being able to hack into the drone surveillance footage gives someone the ability to constantly monitor the status of the home. This leads to significant security issues. Fortifying software defenses is critical to these drones receiving public support. If these issues are remedied, drones may eventually be a more effective and inexpensive method to monitor every corner of the home.

DETECTING DRONE SPIES

With drones becoming increasingly popular, it is hard to differentiate the good from the bad. While some drones are easy to spot in the sky, others are impossible to see. Nighttime conditions, clouds, or altitude

WORDS IN CONTEXT

shroud

To hide from view.

shroud a spying drone from its unsuspecting target. Software engineers and researchers are developing programs to help protect citizens from drone spies in the near future.

Researcher from Israel's Ben-Gurion University (BGU) created a smart film that can be stuck to several types of surfaces. They embedded electronic programming into the film that relays information to a nearby computer. The film actually captures the video feed from the spying drone. This video is downloaded onto the victim's computer as proof of illicit drone usage. BGU also successfully

UNMANNED ENTERTAINERS

While drones have shown many practical uses that help accomplish tasks, they have an underappreciated value–entertainment. During the 2018 Winter Olympic Games opening ceremonies, US viewers were able to watch an aerial light show. The technology company Intel prerecorded a choreographed flight of 1,218 drones. This flight arranged the drones to form the iconic five interconnected Olympic rings. This flight actually earned Intel the Guinness World Records for "most unmanned aerial vehicles airborne simultaneously."

Intel planned to perform a live flight during the ceremonies, but adverse weather conditions forced the show to be grounded. Intel would have flown three hundred drones to arrange the rings, a peace dove, and several other images. The LED lights attached to each drone were able to beam any shape and display 4 billion color combinations. While the cancellation was a disappointment for many, it will not be the last time drones will be used for aerial displays of art.

Quoted in "Drone Light Show from Intel Is Scrapped at Winter Olympics Opening Ceremony," *USA Today*, February 12, 2018. usatoday.com.

attached the film to a white T-shirt, and it successfully worked outdoors and on the go. The BGU team states the program is compatible with close-range laptops.

BGU researcher Ben Nassi believes, "Our findings may help thwart privacy invasion attacks that are becoming more common with increasing drone use."[56] Nassi also says, "This could have significant impact for the military and for consumers because a victim can now legally prove that a neighbor was invading their privacy."[57] An illegal drone operator will soon have to think twice before trying to spy on the community.

THE FUTURE FLIES HIGH

Breakthroughs in the drone industry are making changes in nearly every facet of society. Businesses, militaries, and individuals are tapping into the power of unmanned flight. New examples of futuristic drone use pop up on a regular basis. The progress made since the first drones took flight is astounding.

Drones have proven to be incredibly useful in some applications. They also cause serious problems in the wrong hands. The same drone that delivers products can also deliver injuries. It is up to society and regulatory organizations to ensure the public is getting the most use from these machines while it remains adequately protected.

While drones are common enough to be purchased on store shelves, experts believe we are only scratching the surface of what tomorrow's drones will be capable of. With the technology rapidly advancing and use on the rise, drones are propelling society forward. The ability to look into the future is as simple as looking into the sky.

Source Notes

Introduction: Drones to the Rescue

1. Quoted in Isabella Kwai, "A Drone Saves Two Swimmers in Australia," *New York Times*, January 18, 2018. www.nytimes.com.

2. Quoted in Kwai, "A Drone Saves Two Swimmers in Australia."

3. Quoted in Richard Verrier, "Drones Are Providing Film and TV Viewers a New Perspective on the Action," *Los Angeles Times*, October 8, 2015. www.latimes.com.

4. Quoted in Allen L. Roland, "America's Love Affair with Dark Side—Drone Attacks," *Veterans Today*, January 11, 2015. www.veteranstoday.com.

5. Quoted in Daisy Carrington, "15 Ways Drones Will Change Your Life," *CNN*, November 18, 2013. www.cnn.com.

Chapter 1: What Is the Technology Behind Drones?

6. Quoted in Chelsea Leu, "The Secret History of World War II-Era Drones," *Wired*, December 16, 2015. www.wired.com.

7. Quoted in University of South Florida, "USF Deploys Unmanned Aerial Vehicles to Katrina Rescue Operation," *ScienceDaily*, September 8, 2005. www.sciencedaily.com.

8. Quoted in Matthew Hutson, "Hurricanes Show Why Drones Are the Future of Disaster Relief," *NBC News*, September 9, 2017. www.nbcnews.com.

9. Quoted in Chris Anderson, "Seeing Is Believing: Drones—What Are They Good For?" *Economist*, June 10, 2017. www.economist.com.

10. Quoted in Rob Matheson, "Hybrid Drones Carry Heavier Payloads for Greater Distances," *MIT Mech E*, August 3, 2017, meche.mit.edu.

11. Quoted in Matheson, "Hybrid Drones Carry Heavier Payloads for Greater Distances."

12. Quoted in Iain Thomson, "US Military Drone Goes AWOL, Ends Up Crashing into Tree 623 Miles Away," *Register*, March 2, 2017. www.theregister.co.uk.

13. Quoted in Will Nicholls, "Using Drones to Shoot War Zones," *PetaPixel*, February 20, 2018. petapixel.com.

14. Quoted in Todd Bishop, "Bill Gates: Jeff Bezos Overly Optimistic on Drones, but They Will Have a Positive Impact," *GeekWire*, December 4, 2013. www.geekwire.com.

Chapter 2: Where Are Drones Found Today?

15. Quoted in David Reid, "Domino's Delivers World's First Ever Pizza by Drone," *CNBC*, November 16, 2016. www.cnbc.com.

16 Quoted in Reid, "Domino's Delivers World's First Ever Pizza by Drone."

17. Quoted in Alexandra Genova, "How Drones Are Changing Our View of the World," *Time*, November 18, 2016. time.com.

18. Quoted in Sahil Patel, "Eye in the Sky: Fox Sports Is Bringing Drones to Sporting Events," *Digiday*, June 3, 2016. digiday.com.

19. Quoted in Patel, "Eye in the Sky: Fox Sports Is Bringing Drones to Sporting Events."

20. Quoted in Lee Green, "Legal Issues Related to Use of Drones in High School Sports," *NFHS*, November 21, 2014. www.nfhs.org.

21. Quoted in Ilyce Glink, "9 Ways Drones Are Changing Real Estate," *CBS*, March 6, 2017. www.cbsnews.com.

22. Quoted in Glink, "9 Ways Drones Are Changing Real Estate."

23. Quoted in Glink, "9 Ways Drones Are Changing Real Estate."

24. Quoted in Jeremiah Johnson, "Drones Take Off for Utilities," *Electrical Light and Power*, January 17, 2017. www.elp.com.

25. Quoted in Johnson, "Drones Take Off for Utilities."

26. Quoted in Michael V. Hayden, "To Keep America Safe, Embrace Drone Warfare," *New York Times*, February 19, 2016. www.nytimes.com.

27. Quoted in Kate Baggaley, "Drones Are Setting Their Sights on Wildlife," *Popular Science*, February 10, 2017. www.popsci.com.

Chapter 3: What Are the Risks and Drawbacks of Drones?

28. Quoted in Michael Goldstein, "With First Commercial Air Collision, Is a Drone Disaster Inevitable?" *Forbes*, October 18, 2017. www.forbes.com.

29. Quoted in Goldstein, "With First Commercial Air Collision, Is a Drone Disaster Inevitable?"

30. Quoted in Ben Popper, "Man Gets 30 Days in Jail for Drone Crash That Knocked Woman Unconscious," *Verge*, February 27, 2017. www.theverge.com.

31. Quoted in Courtney Thompson, "Drones Are Reportedly Spying on Women in Australia," *New York Post*, November 3, 2017. nypost.com.

Source Notes Continued

32. Quoted in Thompson, "Drones Are Reportedly Spying on Women in Australia."

33. Quoted in David Barrett, "Burglars Use Drone Helicopters to Target Homes," *Telegraph*, May 18, 2015. www.telegraph.co.uk.

34. Quoted in Barrett, "Burglars Use Drone Helicopters to Target Homes."

35. Paul Mozur, "Drone Maker D.J.I. May Be Sending Data to China, U.S. Officials Say," *New York Times*, November 29, 2017. www.nytimes.com.

36. Quoted in Mozur, "Drone Maker D.J.I. May Be Sending Data to China, U.S. Officials Say."

37. Quoted in Mozur, "Drone Maker D.J.I. May Be Sending Data to China, U.S. Officials Say."

38. Quoted in Sean Higgins, "FBI: Terrorists Expected to Use Aerial Drones Imminently," *Washington Examiner*, September 27, 2017. www.washingtonexaminer.com.

39. Quoted in Higgins, "FBI: Terrorists Expected to Use Aerial Drones Imminently."

40. Quoted in Geneva Sands, "Homeland Security Bulletin Warns of Weaponized Drones and Threat to Aviation," *ABC*, November 9, 2017. abcnews.go.com.

41. David Hastings Dunn, "Small Drones and the Use of Chemical Weapons as a Terrorist Threat," *University of Birmingham*, n.d. www.birmingham.ac.uk.

42. Dunn, "Small Drones and the Use of Chemical Weapons as a Terrorist Threat."

43. Chris Weller, "Drones Could Replace $127 Billion Worth of Human Labor," *Business Insider*, May 11, 2016. www.businessinsider.com.

44. Quoted in Haley Ritchie, "Drones Disturbing Eagles," *Squamish Chief*, November 29, 2017. www.squamishchief.com.

45. Quoted in Ritchie, "Drones Disturbing Eagles."

46. Quoted in Lauren Prince, "Kentucky Man Arrested After Shooting Down Neighbor's Drone," *NBC*, August 1, 2015. www.nbcnews.com.

Chapter 4: What Is the Future of Drones?

47. Evan Ackerman, "EPFL's Collapsable Delivery Drone Protects Your Package with an Origami Cage," *IEEE Spectrum*, September 14, 2017. spectrum.ieee.org.

48. Quoted in “Drone On: Things May Be Looking Up for Delivery of Medical Supplies,” *Mayo Clinic*, April 7, 2015. intheloop.mayoclinic.org.

49. Quoted in Chanapa Tantibanchachai, “Drone Carrying Blood Samples Travels 160 Miles in Arizona Desert to Set New Record,” *Hub*, September 19, 2017. hub.jhu.edu.

50. Quoted in Clinton Nguyen, “Fresh Emergency Organs May Soon Be Delivered by Medical Drones,” *Business Insider*, May 4, 2016. www.businessinsider.com.

51. Quoted in Crystal Ponti, “Rise of the Robot Bees: Tiny Drones Turned into Artificial Pollinators,” *National Public Radio*, March 3, 2017. www.npr.org.

52. Quoted in “Replicating Peregrine Falcon Attack Strategies Could Help Down Rogue Drones,” *University of Oxford: News and Events*, December 5, 2017. www.ox.ac.uk.

53. Quoted in “Replicating Peregrine Falcon Attack Strategies Could Help Down Rogue Drones.”

54. Quoted in “Replicating Peregrine Falcon Attack Strategies Could Help Down Rogue Drones.”

55. Quoted in Andrew J. Hawkins, “Ehang’s Passenger-Carrying Drones Look Insanely Impressive in First Test Flights,” *Verge*, February 5, 2018. www.theverge.com.

56 Quoted in American Associates, Ben-Gurion University of the Negev, “New Method to Detect Illicit Drone Filming Developed,” *ScienceDaily*, January 15, 2018. www.sciencedaily.com.

57. Quoted in “New Method to Detect Illicit Drone Filming Developed.”

For Further Research

Books

Ayperi Karabuda Ecer, *Dronescapes: The New Aerial Photography from Dronestagram*. London: Thames & Hudson, 2017.

Hugh Gusterson, *Drone: Remote Control Warfare*. Cambridge, MA: MIT Press, 2016.

Adam Juniper, *The Complete Guide to Drones: Build, Choose, Fly, Photograph*. London: ILEX, 2015.

Adam Juniper, *Drone Pilot's Handbook*. London: Octopus Publishing Group, 2016.

Stuart A. Kallen, *What Is the Future of Drones?* San Diego, CA: ReferencePoint, 2017.

Carla Mooney, *Careers If You Like Video Games*. San Diego, CA: ReferencePoint, 2018.

Internet Sources

Rob Matheson, "Hybrid Drones Carry Heavier Payloads for Greater Distances," *MechE*, August 3, 2017. meche.mit.edu.

Chanapa Tantibanchachai, "Drone Carrying Blood Samples Travels 160 Miles in Arizona Desert to Set New Record," *Hub*, September 19, 2017. hub.jhu.edu.

Websites

Dronestagram
www.dronestagr.am

Dronestagram is an online art gallery featuring works created using drones. Visitors can view, submit, and rank images and videos captured by drones.

Dronethusiast
www.dronethusiast.com

The Dronethusiast website offers latest news, reviews, tips, and videos about drones. The site also offers tutorials on purchasing and flying drones.

Federal Aviation Administration: Unmanned Aircraft Systems
www.faa.gov/uas

This is the United States FAA website regarding drone usage. The website provides comprehensive information about appropriate and safe drone use. It also offers contact information for people seeking answers from the authority on flight regulation.

How Drones Work
https://science.howstuffworks.com

This HowStuffWorks webpage is an excellent resource for those who wish to explore more about how drones operate in the world today. Information includes history and current drone science and technology. The site also includes links to sites with further information.

MyFirstDrone
https://myfirstdrone.com

MyFirstDrone is a great starting place for anyone interested in purchasing a drone. The site offers useful advice for beginner, intermediate, and advanced drone operators.

Index

Index Continued

Image Credits

Cover: © Jag_cz/Shutterstock Images

4: © Everett Historical/Shutterstock Images

5: © dvande/Shutterstock Images

7: © Halfpoint/Shutterstock Images

9: © donvictorio/Shutterstock Images

10: © A_Lesik/Shutterstock Images

13: © 4 PM production/Shutterstock Images

14: © Everett Historical/Shutterstock Images

16: © motive56/Shutterstock Images

19: © Carla Thomas/AFRC/NASA

27: © Tatiana Chekryzhova/Shutterstock Images

30: © byvalet/Shutterstock Images

35: © Busara/Shutterstock Images

43: © Photo_works/Shutterstock

49: © Minerva Studio/Shutterstock Images

54: © Frederic Legrand - COMEO/Shutterstock Images

58: © Peter Titmuss/Shutterstock Images

61: © Jack Hong/Shutterstock Images

64: © John Locher/AP Images

67: © Dmitry Kalinovsky/Shutterstock Images

About the Author

John Hakala is a freelance writer from Minnesota. Before pursuing a life of writing, he was a nuclear medicine technologist and has published research in the *Journal of Nuclear Medicine Technology*. He currently travels with his wife, Heidi. John is the chief contributor for the blog *Liberty by Choice*.